QUESTAR PUBLISHERS, INC.
SISTERS, OREGON

WHAT WOULD JESUS DO?

An adaptation for children
of Charles M. Sheldon's
IN HIS STEPS

Text by **Mack Thomas**

Illustrations by **Denis Mortenson**

WHAT WOULD JESUS DO?

published by Gold'n'Honey Books
a part of the Questar publishing family

© 1991 by Questar Publishers, Inc.

International Standard Book Number: 0-945564-05-8
Printed in the United States of America

Most Scripture quotations are from the *New International Version*
© 1973, 1984 by International Bible Society
used by permission of Zondervan Publishing House

For information:
QUESTAR PUBLISHERS, INC.
POST OFFICE BOX 1720
SISTERS, OREGON 97759

93 94 95 96 97 98 99 00 01 — 15 14 13 12 11 10 9 8 7 6

*This story happened long ago,
and could happen again—
perhaps very soon...*

1

THE
VISITOR

Hooray, hooray!
Today was the day
for the Valley Church
Rally Day Picnic.

And nearly everyone was there!

While the men were roasting the meat,
the ladies were busy with all the rest—
everything tasty and everything sweet!
And they kept a close eye
on their babies nearby.

The biggest boys had a ball-game going,

while in the gazebo the big girls were showing
their dresses and smiles and Sunday hairstyles.

And at the edge of the Woodsy Woods,
Parson Henry called to the children *your* age:
"Come on! Let's take a walk through the trees,
and keep our eyes wide open! Just maybe we'll spot
a deer or a fox or a Woodsy What-not!"
All the children laughed.

Not far from the church, the Valley Road passed by.
Today, a blue-capped boy came running down it.
His face was dirty, his eyes looked hurt,
and his shirt was torn. He was crying—
not for himself, but for a friend who needed help.

And then—through his tears
he saw the happy picnic crowd, and prayed:
"Lord Jesus, please show me someone there
who will help us—just as *You* would help us
if *You* were here."

*(For this and all the other chapters in this book, you will find
"Questions to Talk About Together" beginning on page 245.)*

2

A TOUGH TIME

The dirty-faced, blue-capped boy walked closer to the picnic...

He came to the men at the roasting fires,
and said, "May I please have water to wash in?
And I have a friend who—"

But they hurried him off to the ladies.

So he asked the ladies, "May I please
have water to wash in? And I have a friend who—"

"Run along now, *run along!*" they answered.
And their babies cried.

The boy ran to the ball-game—
but no one noticed him there.

And at the gazebo, the girls would only stare at the dirty-faced, blue-capped boy.

Into the Woodsy Woods he wandered.
He sat down to rest…and to cry.

Suddenly—close by—he heard a glad sound.
It was a song:

"We have decided to follow Jesus,
We have decided to follow Jesus,
We have decided to follow Jesus,
in every way, and every day."

The song quickly stopped when the Parson
and the children saw the boy. *Who was this?*

3

HARD QUESTIONS

Two children came over
for a closer look—
a girl named Claire
and a boy named Bill...

"Are you a Woodsy What-not?" asked Claire.
But Bill said, "No, he's a boy.
He's dirty—and he may be hurt."

Then the Parson called,
"Bill and Claire! Time to eat!"
"Hooray!" said Bill. "Let's go!" said Claire.

"Please wait!" said the dirty-faced, blue-capped boy.
"Tell me this before you go: I heard you singing
about *Jesus*. Do *you* know Jesus?

"And I wonder: The other people at the picnic—
Do they know Jesus too? And if they do,
why wouldn't they help me when I asked them to?
I only wanted water to wash in,
and some help for a friend.
If I had asked *Jesus*...what would *He* do?"

The Parson and the children didn't know what to say.
The boy walked slowly back to the road.

"Well, shake me awake—we've made a mistake!"
the Parson said, tapping his head.

He called out, "Bill!
Please hurry to find an extra shirt! And Claire,
please get a bucket of water and soap.
I hope we can catch him—I hope, I hope…"

So off they ran—
with the shirt and the water and the soap.

4

NEW
FRIENDS

When they found the boy,
they helped him get clean
and asked him his name...

"I'm Jack," said the blue-capped, clean-faced boy.
Parson Henry smiled.
"So tell me, Jack,
about your friend:
What does he need?
How can we help?"

"Follow me," said Jack, leading the way.
The Parson and Claire and Bill were right behind.
And what did they find?

They found Jack's friend.
Jack said, "His name is Mister Manning.
He can't see, and he can't walk
without his cane.

"And while we were walking today he fell.
His cane dropped into that ditch full of thorns.
I climbed down to find it, but all I got
was dirty and torn."

Then Mister Manning called,
"I hear you, Jack! Welcome back!
And who are the friends you've brought?"
Jack answered, "Parson Henry, and Claire,
and Bill. They helped me wash
and gave me a new shirt.
Wasn't that *swell?*"

"*Well-l-l-l,*" smiled Mister Manning,
"that reminds me of a time the Bible talks about:
Jesus' friends had gathered to eat...
but they had *dirty feet!* No one would wash them.
So what did Jesus do?

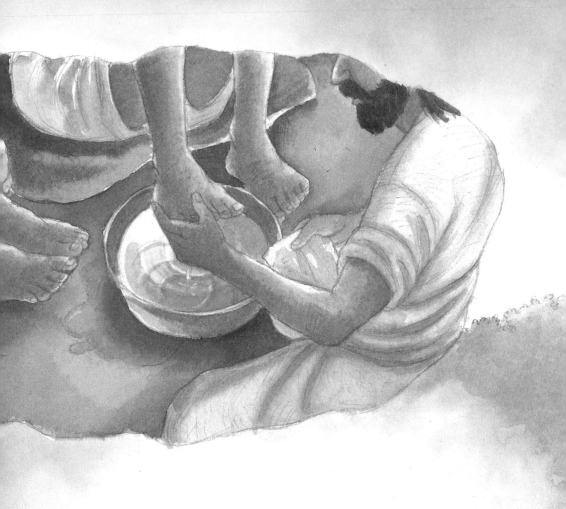

"He took water and washed them—
all those *dirty feet!*
And He said, 'This is My example:
Help one another, just as I help you;
serve one another, just as I serve you.'

tell children

49

"And so I'm proud of you for helping Jack—
just like Jesus would!"

When Mister Manning spoke those words,
Claire looked down...
    Bill rubbed his chin...
        and Parson Henry coughed and said,
            "We're glad, too—true as blue!
But we waited much too long to help him,
I'm sorry to say."

Mister Manning gave a nod, and said,
"It's not always easy to do as Jesus would.
But when you do—doesn't it *feel GOOD?*"
"Yes!" replied the children and the Parson.

"So what do we do now?" asked Bill.
"What would *Jesus* do?" said Claire.
Bill glanced into the ditch, and replied,
"I think He would help find Mister Manning's cane!"

So they made themselves into a chain—
Parson Henry gripped Claire,
and Claire gripped Bill,
and Bill gripped Jack,
and Jack went back
down, down to look.

And he found Mister Manning's cane!

Mister Manning waved goodbye and said,
"My dear friends, try *always* to ask
those four special words: *What would Jesus do?*
And if that gets too hard, come back here
and we'll talk. Jack and I take a walk this way
every afternoon."

Jack danced a little step,
and said, "Now don't forget—
What would JESUS do?"

great idea

5

HIGH
HOPES

Claire and the Parson and Bill
ran back to the picnic.

Bill shouted, "Let's hurry!
We should tell the others
what we've learned
about following Jesus!"

At the creek, Claire stopped to watch
the water flowing by. And she said,
"I wonder: Will the other children
want to learn those Four Special Words?"

"Of course they will," said Bill, as they crossed
a farmer's field: "All of us children,
each and every day, will do nothing at all
until *first* we say, *What would Jesus do?*"
Then Bill and Claire made up this rhyme:

When I'm faced with a fear or a bad attitude,
when I want to be angry or worried or rude,
when I don't want to serve, and don't want to love—
when only MYSELF is what I'm thinking of—
right from the start I will ask in my heart,
WHAT WOULD JESUS DO?

At the picnic, they hurried to the table
where the children were having dessert.
Parson Henry said, "You know, children—
it isn't enough
just to *sing* about following Jesus…
It's something we've got to *DO*."

"It's true!" said Bill.
And Claire added, "True as blue!
So listen now, and we'll tell you how:
Each day, in all you do or say,
first ask yourself, *What would Jesus do?*
That's it! Will YOU try it too?"

But all the children wandered away—
some to their mothers, and some to play.
They didn't seem to care about Jesus that day.

6

THE
PROMISE

Bill moaned to the Parson,
"I guess it's no use.
Nobody likes our plan."

Claire was listening nearby,
while jumping rope and counting:
"One, Two—What should we do?"

She heard the Parson's answer: "Maybe so, Bill.
If this is only *our* idea—ours alone—let's throw it out
like an old chicken bone. Unless, of course,
there's *Someone else* to think about..."

Claire kept listening, and jumping, and counting:
"Three, Four—Open that door!
Five, Six—Be quick, be quick."

Bill suddenly gave a shout:
"There IS Someone else—*Jesus!*
This is *His* idea, not ours!
That's why we met Mister Manning and Jack—
so Jesus could teach us how to do what *He* would do.
Now we *must* follow Jesus; let's never turn back!"

"You're right as light," said Parson Henry
with a twinkle in his eye.
"Let's each promise to try it this week.
For seven whole days we'll keep asking,
What would Jesus do?
Claire, will you join us too?"

Claire skipped faster.
"Seven, Eight—I think it's great!
Nine, Ten—Let's all begin!"

So the three partners shook hands,
and sang their promise to one another:
  "We have decided to follow Jesus,
  We have decided to follow Jesus,
  We have decided to follow Jesus,
  no turning back, no turning back..."

As everyone left the picnic,
huge gray clouds
climbed high in the sky.
"Looks like a storm tonight,"
said the Parson.

Up in the trees,
a bluejay and
a squirrel agreed.

7

A FRIGHTFUL STORM

A few dark hours later,
upstairs in his bed—
covered with a sheet
from his feet to his head—
Bill tried to shut out the storm…

But the next thunder blast
was even louder than the last...
CRASH-A-CRACK! BOOM-BOOM!
Rumble-brummmmmmmm! it sounded.
On the window pane, the wind and rain pounded.
Bill said, "I don't like you! Go away!"
But the storm thundered back: *CRASH-A-CRACK!*
BOOM-BOOM! Rumble-brummmmmmm!

Bill threw off the sheet, tumbled to the floor,
and dove under his bed. He called to the storm,
"If you don't stop, then I'll…I'll…I'll…"

CRASH-A-CRACK! BOOM-BOOM!
Rumble-brum-brummmmmmmm!

"I'm afraid," Bill cried.
He squeezed a little further
under his bed—
and felt something
on the floor by his side…

It was the Pocket Picture Bible
that Parson Henry gave him
for his birthday!
He thought about
the Parson and Claire.
He remembered his promise,
with those Four Special Words:
What would Jesus do?

Bill said a prayer,
right there under his bed:
"Lord Jesus, please help me.
What would *You* do in a storm?
Would *You* be afraid?"

In his Pocket Picture Bible,
Bill found a picture
of Jesus on a boat,
with a storm all around.
His friends on the boat were scared—
but not Jesus!
"Don't be afraid!" Jesus said.

CRASH-A-CRACK! BOOM-BOOM!
came the sound again, and it echoed
around Bill's room:
Rumble-brum-brummmmm...
But Bill was still, and said,
"Thank You, Lord Jesus.
I know You love me,
and I know You're here,
so I have nothing to fear."

Bill got back into bed...

and went to sleep.

8

FINDING
A LOST ROPE

At breakfast the next day,
Claire thought about her birthday jump-rope.
Its wooden handles were red
like an apple, shiny and bright.
The rope had cords of yellow and white,
the colors of butter and milk.
It was Claire's best birthday present ever!
And after breakfast
she rushed to her room to get it.
But it wasn't there!

She looked in the back yard.
It wasn't there!

She searched all over the barn. *It wasn't there!*
It wasn't anywhere! It was gone—out of sight.
Then she remembered last night...

The picnic…by the church…Yes, THAT'S where I left it!
She ran to the churchyard.
And what did she see?

Junior Ray Cobb and Michael McCree
were pretending her rope
was a snake in the dirt!

Claire wanted to scream,
"Leave my birthday jump-rope alone!"

But she remembered her promise,
and those Four Special Words:
"What would Jesus do?"

Claire said a prayer:
"If this jump-rope was Yours somehow—
Lord Jesus, what would *You* do now?"

Then she remembered—
yesterday at Sunday school—
when her teacher said this:
"God likes it when we *share* what we have.
Be *happy* to share—that's what the Bible tells us."

Now Claire whispered, "Yes, Lord.
I will share this beautiful birthday jump-rope."

So she joined the boys...

and the jump-rope became a way to climb a tree...

and a line to catch fish in the sea...

and the reins for a team of mighty reindeer…

and a barn to keep them in.

When lunchtime came, the boys had to go.
They called to Claire, "Goodbye!
Thanks for all the fun!"
    And Claire liked her jump-rope
    more than ever.

9

MISS PAGE'S PLAN

In his quiet office
at the quiet church,
Parson Henry was enjoying
an afternoon nap.
At the door there came a tiny *tap-tap-tap.*

The Parson only snored a little more.

So at the door came a louder *RAP-RAP-RAP!*

"Come in!" said the Parson, waking up with a start.
At the door was Miss Page,
the Sunday school teacher.
The Parson greeted her: "Good afternoon!
And what have we here?
Could that be a tear in your eye?"

Miss Page answered softly,
"What I've seen today has made me cry.
I was riding my horse, Dapper Dill.
We climbed Riddle Hill, where I've never been before.

"And this is what I saw:
Everyone there is oh, so poor!
Their houses are old and full of holes;
and so are their clothes!

"But now I have a plan: Another *picnic!*
We'll invite all the people from Riddle Hill.
We'll serve them our finest food,
and give them presents.
Let's do it soon—next Sunday afternoon!
Can we, Parson Henry?"

The Parson replied,
"Oh...No, I don't think so.
We *don't know* those folks on Riddle Hill.
Someday, maybe, we'll do something for them—
but not so soon; not next Sunday afternoon!"

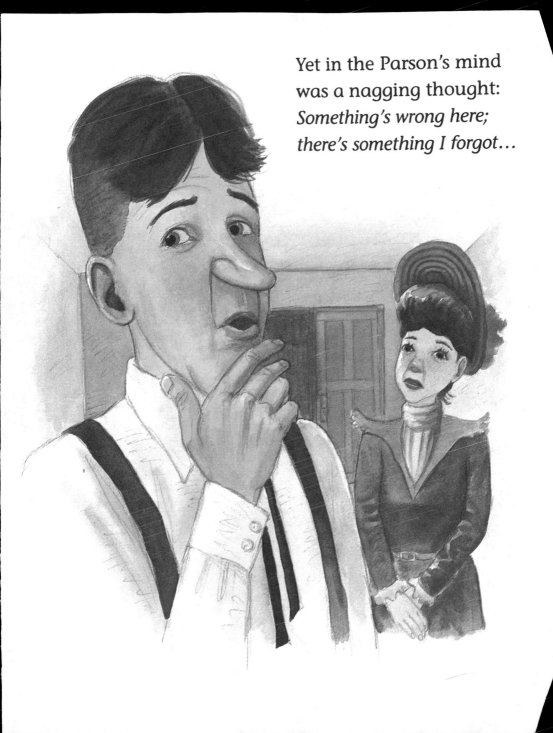

Yet in the Parson's mind
was a nagging thought:
*Something's wrong here;
there's something I forgot...*

Through the window just then came a rowdy sound
from the churchyard. A dog was chasing the squirrel
under Dapper Dill's legs. Dapper didn't like it one bit.
He skittered and jittered and jumped.
And then...

He ran away! "I'll catch Dapper Dill!"
shouted the Parson.
So off after the horse he ran—
still thinking about Miss Page's plan,
and wondering: *What did I forget?*

JACK'S WORDS HELP AGAIN

Across the farmer's field
Parson Henry chased Dapper Dill.
He was saying to himself,
"Another picnic could be fun...

"But I don't think I want to be
with those poor Riddle Hill people.
They're probably dirty, and sick."

On and on and up a hill
the Parson ran after Dapper Dill,
getting closer, and closer, and closer.
"Dapper, stop!" he yelled. "Whoa!"

He came upon the Valley Road, and saw Jack
and Mister Manning out for their afternoon walk.
Dapper Dill was standing at their side.
The men shook hands, and Dapper said *"Neighhhh!"*
The Parson caught his breath,
then finally spoke:
     "My friends—
          how are you today?"

Jack answered, "Mighty swell, Parson!
Mister Manning just told me his favorite Bible stories.
Did you know Jesus loved *everyone?*
Rich people and poor people, clean people
and dirty people, well people and sick people—
He spent time with them all. *That's what Jesus did."*

The Parson dropped his head, and said:
"*Now* I know what I forgot…
I forgot my promise—and four special words:
What would Jesus do?"

The Parson quickly mounted Dapper,
and said, "I must go
and do some planning for a picnic!
Goodbye, Mister Manning!
And goodbye, Jack!
Thank you for reminding me about Jesus."

Down the hill and over the creek
went Dapper Dill and the Parson.

When they reached the farmer's field,
the Parson stopped to pray:
"I'm sorry, Lord Jesus;
I forgot to think about You.
Help me learn
to ask much sooner,
What would Jesus do?"

11

IN A
FIX

Late the next day
Claire came to the churchyard,
hoping to find someone to play with.
There she saw her teacher,
who said, "Hello, Claire."

"Hi, Miss Page! Where are you going,
you and Dapper Dill?"
Miss Page smiled with excitement, and answered:
"Up to Riddle Hill! I'm inviting everyone there
to join us for a big new picnic—
next Sunday afternoon!
The Parson and I were just planning it."

Miss Page leaned closer: "And Claire,
I'm asking each girl and boy in Sunday school
to bring a gift to the picnic—
a favorite toy, or something else you enjoy
but are willing to give to children who are poor."

As Miss Page rode away,
Claire thought about those words:
A favorite toy...something I enjoy...
What I <u>most</u> enjoy is my beautiful birthday jump-rope.
But I can't give <u>that</u> away—can I?
If I did, I know I would never be happy again...

She started jumping:
> *"One, Two*—What should I do
> *Three, Four*—for kids who are poor
> *Five, Six*—at the big picnic?
> *Seven, Eight*—I sure would hate
> *Nine, Ten*—to lose my friend,
> my beautiful birthday jump-rope...
> *Ohhhhh!"*

Even thinking such a thing made Claire feel afraid—
afraid of being unhappy forever.

She stopped to talk to the flowers:
"I suppose I could stay home
from the picnic, and say I was sick.
Or I could hide my rope,
and say it was lost again.
But no—all that would be lying."

Just then, from behind her,
she heard a scary sound.

She turned around.
"Oh, it's only *you*—a squirrel!
I wish you were somebody
I could talk to and play with."

The gray squirrel chattered away:
"Chitta-*chack,* chitta-*chack,* chitta-*chack!*"

"Jack!" Claire suddenly thought;
"and Mister Manning!
I'll go visit them!"

Claire almost started to pray.
And she almost said aloud
those Four Special Words.

But instead,
she bounced away,
gripping her jump-rope
even tighter than before.

CLAIRE'S FEAR

On the Valley Road,
Jack and Mister Manning
sat down to rest.

Just then,
Claire came jumping up
in a cloud of dust...

She said hello,
and sat down beside them.
Then she asked,
"By the way: Do you know
about the new picnic?"
Jack answered,
"Yes, we do! Miss Page let us know
just moments ago."
Claire spoke again:
"Miss Page is asking all of us kids
to give something to the poor Riddle Hill children.
But I don't need to give away my jump-rope, do I?
Don't you think I should keep it for myself?"

Mister Manning replied gently,
"Claire, have you asked,
What would Jesus do?"
Claire cried, "I was *afraid* to,
and afraid to pray.
I don't want to give my jump-rope away!
That would make me *unhappy forever!*"

Suddenly, Mister Manning stood and shouted:
"Let's go on a treasure hunt!"
He stepped out in front,
and Jack and Claire
followed behind.

13

TREASURE
ALL AROUND

"Remember,"
said Mister Manning to Claire,
"my eyes are blind—
so *you* must help me
find the treasure!

"Now tell me what you see: By any chance,
is there a huge blue sky above us,
with a golden sun, and clouds
that look like cotton?
Have we found it?
Is it there?"

"Why, yes, it's there," answered Claire.

Mister Manning continued:
"And now, look around us.
Do beautiful things surround us?
Are there fields and flowers
and water and woods
and rocks and bugs and birds?
Is all of it there?"

"Once again: All there,"
said Claire.

They stopped by a lake.
Mister Manning and Jack took off their shoes.
They splashed their feet in the water,
while Mister Manning said,

"Just think:
Jesus gave us all this treasure.
His gifts to us are everywhere.
And look again! There's more!
Do you see an old blind man
with a girl and boy at his side?
Did you know Jesus *died* for them?
Out of love, He gave His *life*
for that man and boy and girl—
and all the people in the whole, wide world!

"Yes, Claire, Jesus gave us everything He had.
So do you think He's *unhappy?*
Right now, is He *sad?*
Or is Jesus ever-so-joyfully glad?
Do you see His smile in the sunshine?
Can you listen to His laughter in the breeze?
And when you're still—can you hear Him
whispering His love in your heart?"

Quietly, quietly, they listened
to happy sounds in the world Jesus made.

"Mister Manning," whispered Claire,
"I'm ready now to pray:

"Dear Jesus, now I can give away
this beautiful birthday jump-rope.
I know it won't make me sad.
For *You're* still glad,
even though You gave *everything!*
Thank You, Lord Jesus.
Now I truly want to do
what *You* would do."

"You know," said Mister Manning later,
 as he and Jack walked Claire home,
"I know many children who would love
 to share a jump-rope like that!
 These children are poor—and what's more,
 they're my neighbors and friends."
 So Claire said,
"Perhaps *they* should have the jump-rope,
 instead of the Riddle Hill children."
 Mister Manning laughed:
"But they *are* the Riddle Hill children!"
"What do you mean?" asked Claire.

Jack explained it: "Riddle Hill is where
Mister Manning lives—and me too!"
"Oh! I didn't know that!" said Claire.
Jack smiled, "Neither do Bill and the Parson.
And just for fun, let's not tell them yet—
not until Sunday at the picnic!"

So the three shook hands.
Everything was set for a great surprise.

14

DOLLAR DAN'S PLAN

Bill was deep in the woods
the next day, chasing bluejays.
But he quickly stopped
when he heard voices—
boy voices...

Over near a willow tree,
Bill saw three big boys.
This spot looked like their hideout.
Bill wondered if he should leave,
but he told himself,
I'd like to hear
what they're talking about.

Bill crept closer.
He saw Bruno Miller wearing a big new hat.
Dollar Dan Smith was beside him, carving a stick.
And Beany Joe Larsen was looking on, and talking:

"That new picnic at the church sounds great!
Let's get there early so we don't miss any food!"

"Forget it, Beany Joe. I don't think we should go!"
Bruno said.

And Dollar Dan agreed:
"I couldn't stand being near
all those poor people from Riddle Hill.
Anyway, I wish there was something
more exciting around here than a picnic.
I'd like to see a *fight*,
or a *wreck*—or better yet, a *FIRE!*

"Guys! Here's a blazing idea: *Let's visit Riddle Hill!*"

Bruno grumbled at Dan, "But you just said
you didn't like those people!"

Dan grinned: "I don't! So we'll go
when they're not there—next Sunday afternoon!
While everyone is at the picnic,
we'll go to Riddle Hill with matches,
and play a trick."

When Bill heard those mean words,
he thought again about leaving.
Surely that's what Jesus would do, he told himself.
But he still didn't turn to go.
He stayed to hear Beany Joe raise his voice:

"Start a fire on Riddle Hill? That's crazy!
What if you burn down someone's home?"
Dan laughed, "So what?
Their houses are nothing but shacks!
And it's just for *fun!* It won't hurt anyone.
We'll be the only ones there."

"I'll help you, Dan!" said Bruno.
Then Dollar Dan jabbed his finger at Beany Joe.
"And as for *you,* Beany Joe Larsen—
now that you've heard my plan,
you've got to come too!"

Beany Joe stuttered:
"I...I...I'd rather go to the picnic—
but I guess I'll go with you instead."

Just then, Bill's nose told him he had to sneeze.
"Uh...uh...uh...

"Uh-CHOO!" sneezed Bill.

And when he opened his eyes again,
three big boys were staring down at him.

15

A DARK WARNING

Dollar Dan growled at Bill:
"You heard our plan, *didn't you?*
Well don't you *dare* tell anyone!
Or else…

"Or else we'll throw you
down in the Valley Church storm-cellar!
It's dark and damp down there,
and *spiders* and *snakes* live there!
And that's where we'll put you
if you tell anyone our plan!"

The boys let Bill go. And he ran away—
without even thinking first, *What would Jesus do?*
As he ran, he heard the bluejays calling,
"Ka-*cheer,* ka-*cheer,* ka-*cheer!*"
"I'm glad you're here,"
Bill told them.

He met a gray squirrel, too.
"What should I *do?*" Bill said aloud,
wishing the squirrel could answer.
The squirrel only chattered,
"Chitta-*chack,* chitta-*chack,* chitta-*chack!*"
Then Bill spoke again: "I know what I'll do:
I'll go see Jack and Mister Manning!"

Bill pushed through the woods,
and came onto the Valley Road.
There he knew Jack and Mister Manning
would soon be walking by.

But then, in the trees behind him,
he heard voices. *Boy voices...*

It was those three boys!
And Dollar Dan was laughing:
"Don't forget: It's dark down there,
and *spiders* and *snakes* live there—
down in the Valley Church storm-cellar!"

And now—did Bill ask
those Four Special Words?
Did he wait for his friends,
Jack and Mister Manning?
Did he pray, and ask Jesus
to help him be brave?

No…
Bill turned toward home—
and ran.

16

LIGHT OF
THE WORLD

On Saturday morning
the sky was cloudy and dark.
Parson Henry went outdoors
to walk and pray.
There he saw Bill—
sitting and staring
at the storm-cellar door.

"Hello, Bill!" he called...

"Good morning, Parson.
Is that cellar door locked?"

"No, Bill. Do you want in there?"

"*Oh!*...No, not me, Parson.
In fact, maybe it *should* be locked—
right away!"

"Well, Bill, we keep the cellar open
so when terrible windstorms blow,
people can go inside and be safe."

"*Safe?* Is it safe down there, Parson?"

"As safe as anywhere!"

"No spiders and snakes?"

"No snakes that I know of, Bill.
Maybe a spider or two. But I think
a spider is safer than a storm. Don't you?"

"I guess so. But isn't it...isn't it
terribly *dark* down there?"

The Parson whistled, and said, "Dark indeed—
especially in a storm. I was down there once
in the darkest storm I've ever known.
But in that darkness I remembered these words
that Jesus said:

> *'I am the Light of the world,*
> *and whoever follows Me*
> *<u>will never walk in darkness</u>.'*

Bill, no matter how dark it seems,
we really *do* have light, since we have Jesus with us.
Good words to remember, don't you think?"

"I think so, Parson.
May I have a drink?"

The Parson led the way to the well,
and pumped up water for Bill.
Bill took three sips, and then asked,
"Do we know anyone
who lives on Riddle Hill?"
The Parson answered, "Not yet.
But tomorrow we will,
when we meet them all
at the picnic!"

Bill dug his hands into his pockets. "Parson,
if a fire burned all the houses on Riddle Hill—
how much would it matter?
How much should we care?"
The Parson looked closely at his friend.
"Bill...how much would *Jesus* care?"

Before Bill could answer,
rain started to fall.

"Come on inside!" the Parson said.
Bill answered, "No, thanks,
I'll just hurry home."

The Parson said quietly, "Bill, before you go,
is there something you want to tell me?
Something we could pray about together?"
Both of them now
were soaking wet from the rain.
Bill started to speak—but didn't.
He looked back at the cellar door.
It made him feel so afraid!

Bill turned—
and again he ran away.

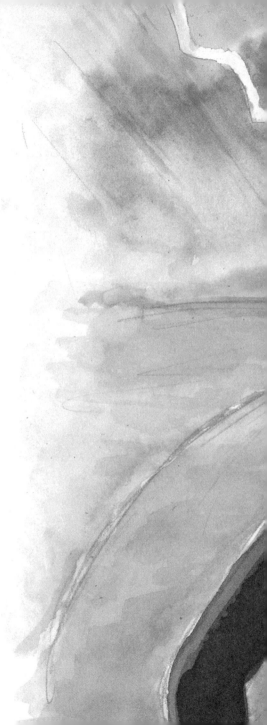

The Parson walked by the cellar door.
There he stopped in the rain, and prayed:
"Lord Jesus, whatever is troubling Bill today,
help him to do as You would do.
Show him the way.
And please don't let him forget
how much You love him."

17

A SHARED
SECRET

All day Saturday
the rain came down.
But Sunday was sunny,
and people came to church
wearing their biggest smiles.

As they thought about the big picnic
to be held that very afternoon,
all the boys and girls in Miss Page's class
were laughing and talking—
all, that is, except Bill.

Claire saw Bill's sadness, and thought,
I know how to make him happy!

That afternoon she found him outside,
where the men were roasting the meat.
"Bill, I have a *secret* to share!
The Riddle Hill people will soon be here,
and guess who'll come with them?
They live at Riddle Hill,
but *we* didn't know it!
I won't make you guess, Bill—
I'll tell you who they are:
Our two *very best* friends,
who taught us to ask,
What would Jesus do? YES!
JACK and MISTER MANNING!"

Claire thought this would make Bill smile.
But instead...

Bill turned away, shouting:
"I'VE GOT TO WARN THEM!"

He was off like a flash—
running faster than ever before.

18

THE
GREAT FIRE

All along the road,
the people of Riddle Hill
were coming to the picnic.
Bill looked at every face.
Where were Mister Manning and Jack?

He finally found them at the very end of the line—
for Mister Manning was slow.

"*Bill!* What's wrong?" asked Jack.

Bill told them everything: "I know three boys
who plan to set fire to Riddle Hill—
today, while everyone is at the picnic!
They said they would throw me in the storm cellar
if I told anyone. But now I don't care!"

Jack gave a cry:

"*Oh, no!* There's *smoke*—right above Riddle Hill!"

Mister Manning quickly gave orders:
"Jack, run as fast as you can to the church.
Tell everyone there that Riddle Hill is on fire.

"Run, Jack! And Bill—you come with me!
We'll go up to Riddle Hill. You will be my eyes."

As they hurried along, Mister Manning asked Bill,
"Did you tell those boys that setting fires is wrong?"

"I could have, Mister Manning;
but instead I ran away."

"Why didn't you come and talk to Jack and me?"

"I tried to, Mister Manning;
but instead I ran away."

"Couldn't you tell Parson Henry what was happening?"

"I wanted to, Mister Manning;
but instead I ran away."

They climbed the dirt road to Riddle Hill.
"What do you see?" asked Mister Manning.

Bill answered,
"Lots and lots of smoke."

They reached the top, and stopped.
"Now what do you see?" Mister Manning asked.
Bill said sadly, "Every home is burning.
The fire and smoke goes higher and higher.
Oh, I'm sorry, Mister Manning!
Your house must be burning too!"

Mister Manning smelled the awful smoke.
He felt the terrible heat.
And he heard the sound of Bill, crying.

Mister Manning spoke softly:
"Bill, how many times did you run away this week?"

"Three times, sir."

"You know, Bill, that reminds me of Peter in the Bible.
He turned away from Jesus *three times*.
But when Peter was sorry,
do you remember what Jesus did?"

"Yes sir. Jesus forgave him."

"That's right, Bill. I know you're sorry
for what *you've* done. And I know
Jesus will forgive you. I forgive you, too.
That's what Jesus would do."

"I'm sorry too,"
a voice cried out behind them.

They turned and saw Beany Joe, who said,
"I came back to stop the burning—but I couldn't.
I know it was wrong to help start the fire. Please help me
learn to do right, and tell me more about Jesus!"
"We will," said Mister Manning.

Then hundreds of people came up the hill,
with a fire-wagon in the lead.
They brought buckets and axes
and shovels to fight the fire.
But it was all too late.

19

UP FROM
THE ASHES

Looking out on the ruins of Riddle Hill,
Parson Henry spoke to the people:
"Some of us here have been learning this week
what it means to follow Jesus.
We're trying to ask in everything,
What would JESUS do?
We've made mistakes, it's true—
and smoke now fills the sky,
and ashes lie all around us...

"The people here who are poorest—
the people of Riddle Hill—
have lost even the little they had.
This is terribly sad. But it's not the end!
Dear friends, I ask YOU:
Right here and right now, what would Jesus do?"

From the crowd of church people
a man's voice sounded:
"He would build new houses—
better houses than before!"
Up rose a cheer from the church people.

"And who will help us build this new Riddle Hill?"
shouted Parson Henry. The first to say "I will!"
were Beany Joe and Bill.
Many others said it, too—both young and old.

The church people made another promise, too:
They decided to share their homes, their food,
and their clothes with the people of Riddle Hill
while the new houses were being built.

So all the people began their new work—
just as Jesus would do.

20

THE
DREAM

In the following days and years,
the Valley Church people gave everything
to make Riddle Hill a new and better place.
Parson Henry, Miss Page, and the others
told all their new friends about Jesus.
They helped build new homes,
and new happiness,
and new hope.

Beany Joe found new friends—good friends—
who helped him do good things.
And his *very best* new friend was Jesus.

Dan and Bruno were sent away for starting the fire.
Bill and Joe went to visit them.
They talked about Jesus and forgiveness.

Jumping with a certain jump-rope
became a favorite game for Riddle Hill children.
Claire came often to play with them,
and had more fun than ever.

And Jack had a special dream.
In his dream he traveled everywhere,
watching and listening.
All over the world
he found churches and homes
where men and women, girls and boys
would always ask: *What would Jesus do?*

When Jack awoke, he prayed:
"Lord Jesus, let this dream come true!"

QUESTIONS
TO TALK ABOUT
TOGETHER

Most Scripture quotations in this section are from
The New Century Version, ©1987 by Worthy Publishing.
Also quoted is *The New International Version,*
© 1973, 1978, 1984 by the International Bible Society.

Chapter 1 — The Visitor

- Do you remember what the men were doing at the picnic? How about the ladies? And all the children?
- What did the blue-capped boy ask Jesus to do for him?
- Can you tell about a time when you asked Jesus to help you?
- The blue-capped boy had a friend who needed help. Do you have any friends who need help?

Chapter 2 — A Tough Time

- What song were the children and the Parson singing (on page 26)? Do you know this song?
- In the last chapter, the blue-capped boy prayed to Jesus. In this prayer he asked Jesus to show him someone who could help him. Has Jesus answered that prayer yet?
- What do you think will happen next?

Chapter 3 — Hard Questions

- What did the blue-capped boy say to Bill and Claire and the Parson?
- The Parson told Bill and Claire, "We've made a mistake." What mistake did they make?
- Here's a good verse to learn and remember: "If we obey what God has told us to do, then we are sure that we truly know God" (1 John 2:3).

Chapter 4 — New Friends

- Do you remember the prayer Jack prayed in the first chapter? (If not, look back at page 17.) How has Jesus answered that prayer?
- What does it mean to "serve one another" (as Mister Manning talks about on page 49)?
- What four special words did Mister Manning and Jack tell the children and the Parson not to forget?

Chapter 5 — High Hopes

- What have we learned in this chapter that we can do when we don't feel like following Jesus?
- Which is easier: singing about following Jesus, or really *doing* the things Jesus wants us to do? Which will make us feel more glad?
- For fun, go back and read together again the rhyme Bill and Claire made up (you'll find it on page 63). Do these words sound like the way *you* are sometimes?

Chapter 6 — The Promise

- *Who* wants us to do what Jesus would do?
- What did Bill and Claire and the Parson promise one another?
- What song did they sing? (Look at it together again, on page 75. You may want to sing it together too!)
- The last words in their song were these: "No turning back, no turning back." What do these words mean?
- Why do you think Jesus wants us to follow Him?

Chapter 7 — A Frightful Storm

- Have you been in any storms like this one? If so, what was it like?
- What did Bill pray, and how did Jesus answer his prayer?
- What was in the picture Bill found in his Pocket Picture Bible? Do you know the Bible story that goes with that picture? (You'll find it in Matthew 8:23-27. Look also at Matthew 14:22-27, especially Jesus' words in verse 27.)

Chapter 8 — Finding a Lost Rope

- What were the boys doing with Claire's jump-rope?
- When Claire saw this, what did she feel like doing? What did she do instead?
- When Claire shared her jump-rope with the boys, they did lots of fun things with it. Could Claire have done these same things all by herself?
- Just as Claire shared her rope, name some things that you can share with others.

Chapter 9 — Miss Page's Plan

- What did Miss Page see at Riddle Hill?
- Miss Page has a plan for helping the poor people of Riddle Hill. What is her plan? Do you think Jesus would like it?
- What important words has the Parson forgotten?

Chapter 10 — Jack's Words Help Again

- Do you know some Bible stories that show us how Jesus loves everyone? (You can find some in Luke 15:1-7, Luke 18:15-17, Matthew 9:10-13, and Mark 1:40-42.)
- What did the Parson do when he remembered what he had forgotten? What can *we* do when we know we have forgotten to do what Jesus would do?
- How will Jesus help us learn to follow Him?

Chapter 11 — In a Fix

- How does Claire feel about giving away her jump-rope? Why do you think she feels this way?
- Are you happy when you give a gift to someone? (Jesus once said, "It is more blessed to give than to receive"—*Acts 20:35*).
- Why do you think Claire didn't ask herself the Four Special Words?

Chapter 12 — Claire's Fear

- Claire told Mister Manning she was afraid. Does Jesus want us to be afraid? (A verse to think about as you answer: Jesus said in Luke 12:32, "Do not be afraid, little flock.")
- Should we ever be afraid of praying? (In 1 Thessalonians 5:17 we read this: "Never stop praying.")
- Mister Manning is leading Jack and Claire on a treasure hunt. Have you ever been on a treasure hunt? If so, what was it like?

Chapter 13 — Treasure All Around

- What kind of treasure did Mister Manning show Claire?
- Why has Jesus given us so much?
- Why did Jesus die for us? (The Bible answers that question in John 3:16—"For God loved the world so much that he gave his only Son. God gave his Son so that whoever believes in him may not be lost, but have eternal life.")
- Where do Jack and Mister Manning live?

Chapter 14 — Dollar Dan's Plan

- What is Dollar Dan's plan, and why is it wrong?
- Psalm 119:60 is a Bible verse that tells us how good it is to obey God's commands *quickly:* "I hurried and did not wait to obey your commands." Has Bill obeyed God quickly?
- What do you think Bill should do now?

Chapter 15 — A Dark Warning

- What does it mean to be *brave?* Is Bill being brave? Who can help *us* be brave?
- What would you do now if you were Bill?
- Can you think of some ways that Bill could find help now to do the right thing?

Chapter 16 — Light of the World

- What is Bill afraid of? If Bill had told the Parson about his fear, how could the Parson have helped him?
- When the Parson prayed for Bill, he said to Jesus, "Help Bill do as You would do. Show him the way." Do you know someone you could pray this good prayer for?
- Do you think Bill understands how much Jesus loves him?

Chapter 17 — A Shared Secret

- All the children in Miss Page's class were happy except Bill. Why wasn't Bill happy?
- Why did Bill turn and run when Claire shared her secret?
- What do you hope will happen next?

Chapter 18 — The Great Fire

- Is Bill sorry for what he has done? What is Bill learning?
- Beany Joe wants to learn about how to do right. He also wants to learn more about Jesus. If you were Mister Manning or Bill, what would you tell Beany Joe about doing right? What would you tell him about Jesus?
- What does the word *forgive* mean? When we do something wrong, does Jesus want to forgive us? (Look together at 1 John 1:9.)

Chapter 19 — Up from the Ashes

- Who is going to help build new houses for the Riddle Hill people?
- What are the Valley Church people learning about how to follow Jesus?
- What are *you* learning about how to follow Jesus day by day?

Chapter 20 — The Dream

- What do you think Bill and Joe told Dan and Bruno when they visited them?
- Why is Claire happy now?
- What was Jack's special dream? Do you want his dream to come true? What could you do to help this dream come true?

MORE GOLD'N'HONEY BOOKS

IN HIS HANDS
The Continuing Adventures of *What Would Jesus Do?*
Retold from Charles Sheldon's classic *In His Steps*

Written by MACK THOMAS / Illustrations by 'MAGINATION

Like the award-winning *What Would Jesus Do?*, this sequel is a special retelling for children of Charles M. Sheldon's immortal *In His Steps*, the all-time bestselling Christian novel. The final portion of that work—in which the scene shifts from a Midwestern town to the clashing worlds of rich and poor in Chicago in the 1890s—provides the inspiration for *In His Hands*. Bringing the story alive are 140 full-color illustrations, plus discussion questions in the back of the book for each of the eighteen chapters.

THE BEGINNER'S BIBLE
TIMELESS CHILDREN'S STORIES

THIS #1 CHILDREN'S BESTSELLER has more than 500 color illustrations and 95 stories (from both Old and New Testaments), all in a durable book perfectly sized for little hands and laps.

> "It's all here and it's all in order—advanced theology in living color and captivating characters. The stories speak for themselves, but kids will want to hear them over and over again. More than just 'stories,' these words and pictures will become part of your child's life."
>
> — JONI EARECKSON TADA

> "*THE BEGINNER'S BIBLE* is in a class all its own. I've never seen Bible text and illustrations come together with such magical quality. This is the Bible to help every young child vividly experience God's truth. I wish Norma and I had it when our kids were small. We'll certainly make sure it's available to our future grandkids!"
>
> — GARY SMALLEY